SOMETH
PREACH

12 DISCIPLESHIP MESSAGES

To encourage you in your walk with Jesus

BY JIM COLLINS

Copyright © Jim Collins

The right of Jim Collins to be identified as author of this work has been asserted by him in accordance with the Copyright, Designs and Patents Act 1988

Published in 2023 by Verité CM for Jim Collins

All Rights Reserved. No part of this publication may be reproduced or transmitted in any form or by any means, electronic or mechanical including photocopying, recording, or any information storage and retrieval system, without permission in writing from the author.

Biblical quotations are taken from the Holy Bible, New International Version, © 1973, 1978, 1984 International Bible Society, used by permission of Zondervan Bible Publishers.

Other Biblical quotations are from the Holy Bible, New International Version. © 1978 by New York International Bible Society.

ESV – English Standard Version – © 2001 by Crossway, a publishing ministry of Good News Publishers

The Message – The New Testament, Psalms and Proverbs – © 1993, 1994, 1995, 1996 by Eugene H. Peterson.

NLT – The New Living Translation, © 1996, 2004 by Tynedale Charitable Trust.

The Amplified Bible – © 1954, 1958, 1962, 1964, 1965, 1987 by The Lockman Foundation.

The Applied New Testament Commentary – © 1996 Thomas Hale and 1996 Stephen Thorson.

The Applied Old Testament Commentary – © 2007 Thomas Hale and 2007 Stephen Thorson.

Please note – Italics within scriptures quoted and the general text are 'emphasis added' by the author.

ISBN: 978-1-914388-40-8

Cover design, typesetting and production management by Verité CM Ltd, Worthing, West Sussex UK +44 (0) 1903 241975

Printed in England

Contents

Foreword

We first met Jim nearly 10 years ago when we moved to Dartmouth to lead the Flavel Church. Jim's regular visits to preach and lead worship have been a great source of encouragement to us as a church community and his enthusiasm for the gospel is infectious.

In this book, Jim's use of roads and other analogies are very apt. We were reminded of sponsored church coastal walks as a child. Everyone would start out on the journey with enthusiasm and lots of energy. However, at points along the journey the energy levels waned a bit, and it seemed like the destination was still far off and the journey never ending. We were sustained on our way by the checkpoints, the encouragements, the refreshments and the cheery words to spur us on. There were the steep ascents over headlands and the long windy pathways down into the valleys and coves. The awesome views, the inspiring sights and the wonders of nature made the trek easier. Keeping our eyes firmly fixed on our destination and reaching our goal kept us motivated.

We pray that, in the same way, Jim's book will encourage us all, whether we are embarking on this exciting adventure for the first time as eager novices, or as we are continuing our discipleship journey after many years, as experienced travellers. As we face the inevitable challenges but also the joys, as we struggle with the difficulties but also are inspired by this amazing journey, may we keep our eyes fixed on

Jesus each step of the way, knowing that he is our role model, friend and the reason for our journey in the first place!

As Jim points out in the book, we should always stay open to learning new things about God which will help us as disciples and disciplers of others. If we think we know all there is to know, that is a dangerous place to be, as our journey of understanding and revelation continues until we finally come face to face with Jesus!

As we seek to be more like Jesus and to focus on our final destination, books like this one encourage us on our walk and remind us that the path we have taken is the only one worth following. (John 14:6)

The practical applications Jim includes at the end of each section will be a useful tool for us to apply on each of our discipleship journeys whether individually or with a group of fellow travellers!

Deborah and Karl Stone
Local Church Leaders – at Flavel Church,
Dartmouth, Devon.

Introduction

At this time of writing, I have had the privilege and opportunity of preaching the Word of God within many Churches and denominations – for just over 40 years.

I recall my earliest message given to a small Baptist fellowship in Christow, Devon, when I spoke on 'The Grace of our Lord Jesus Christ, the Love of God our Father and the Fellowship of the Holy Spirit.'

Looking back, I am so grateful to the many congregations that were supportive, encouraging, and appreciative of my ministry – especially in the early years when I was gaining confidence in proclaiming and expounding God's Word.

I continue to be a learner and desire to remain teachable, as I continue to build up the Body of Christ (His Church) through sharing God's commands, promises and blessings that are found in the Bible.

One of the key scriptures that has kept me faithful in the ministry of God's Word to others, is the command from Jesus, found in the Great Commission verses in Matthew 28:19. "Therefore go and make disciples of all nations…"

As the years fly by, and the Day of the Lord's Second Coming draws closer, I sense the urgency in ensuring that Christians continue to grow in their love for Jesus – and from our love for Him, we serve Him and others.

In Acts 14:21-22, we read how Paul and Barnabas preached the good news in Derbe and won a large number of disciples and then returned to Lystra, Iconium and Antioch, strengthening and encouraging the disciples to remain true to the faith.

In my messages, I seek to enable followers of Jesus to stay close to Him in every situation of life, to keep pressing on towards the goal of our high calling in Christ and remaining faithful to the truth of God's Word.

For this, my latest publication – I have called it 'Something To Preach About.'

The word preach means to proclaim, to declare and announce. Jesus said to His disciples, "Go into all the world and preach the good news to all creation." (Mark 16:15) Paul instructed Timothy – "Preach the Word; be prepared in season and out of season; correct, rebuke and encourage – with great patience and careful instruction." (2 Timothy 4:2)

In the chapters of this book, I aim to declare and announce to you – the life changing Good News of Jesus Christ, and His call to side with Him and be His disciple.

There is an additional message to conclude – called 'Words for the Journey.' This high-lights some of the discipleship lessons (outlined in this book) – that came to my mind during the times of lock-down due to the Covid 19 pandemic.

Discipleship is a life-time walk and journey of becoming more like Jesus, being changed from one degree of glory to another. It will end when we meet Jesus face to face for "we know that when He appears, we shall be like Him, for we shall see Him as He is." (1 John 3:2b)

Discipleship is an amazing and exciting journey, but also a challenging path of faith in God – as Jesus continues to teach us His ways of how to live, love, forgive, trust – and empower us to be His witnesses to share the Good News of the gospel in faith and works.

To reinforce the journey aspect of discipleship, the message themes are linked with roads or paths that we walk on in every-day life. (E.g., track, trail, pathway …)

There are of course many other aspects to our walking as a disciple of Jesus, but I hope these key topics selected for this book, will help inspire, correct, and guide you on your journey of faith and trust in Jesus.

At times, the messages remain in note format – with a good number of scriptures for you to consider and study further on your own, or within a small group discussion. These lessons in discipleship are written as sermons for Church services – so the topics are certainly not exhaustive or conclusive in their content.

You will find it helpful, if you read the full scripture passage given under the sermon title.

Like most preachers, I recommend that listeners (and readers) continue to search out the scriptures for themselves.

I have added a 'Reflection for prayer and action' at the end of each message. One of the main questions I ask a congregation when I preach is; – "What will we do with what we've heard today?" It is vital that what we hear – and read – does not just become information.

Take some time to quietly reflect and pray after each chapter and ask the Holy Spirit to speak to your heart and mind. Consider this question. "Is there anything I need to do today, in obedience to God's Word?"

May you know the continued grace, strength, and presence of Jesus as you walk with Him.

Jim Collins

The Road of Reconciliation

Reading – 2 Corinthians 5:11-21

As a disciple and follower of Jesus Christ we have been reconciled to God. Our sins have been forgiven and we experience the peace and joy of living in right relationship with a Holy God.

The Dictionary definition of the word reconciliation is to bring back into friendship and acceptance – to harmonize. A reunion.

I have a fond memory of when I had a reunion with the Band members of the group 'Exodus' which I used to play guitar for – when I was aged 17. We got together for the 50th birthday of our drummer – to play at his party. It was a great time of renewing friendship and performing music again after over 30 years of not playing together.

The Bible holds the key to the most amazing story of reconciliation that is available to everyone. *The Road of Reconciliation starts at the Cross of Christ.*

The Good News of the gospel is that God is in the business of reconciling sinful people to Himself – the One and only Holy God. Isaiah (59:2) says "...your iniquities have separated you from God; your sins have hidden His face from you..."

Both the root and the result of sin is a broken relationship with God.

The sin-factor that separates us from God – has been dealt

with, – because the death of Jesus on the Cross paying the price for our sinfulness, means we can experience restored relationship with God.

One of images we can use to remind ourselves of the reconciliation that God has provided for us, is in the home-coming of the prodigal son. (See Luke 15:11-24) Like this lost son, we can come back to our Father God and experience His love, forgiveness, and blessing as He welcomes us home.

Ephesians 2:13 reminds us "…now in Christ, you who once were far away have been brought near through the blood of Christ." The Message Bible says, "Now because of Christ – dying that death, shedding that blood – you who were once out of it altogether are in on everything."

The Road of Reconciliation was laid at a great cost.

I recall the local 'Kingsteignton By-Pass' (now the A380 South Devon Highway which opened in 2016) was delayed being constructed for many years with the financial cost – being a key factor.

In contrast; the cost of the Road of Reconciliation was paid by God's love, amazing grace, tender mercy, and the life-blood of His Son Jesus – just for you!

Colossians 1:19-20 tells us – "For God was pleased to have all His fullness dwell in Him (Christ) and through Him to reconcile to himself all things, whether things on earth or things in heaven, by making peace through His blood, shed on the cross."

The Road of Reconciliation leads us to a place of belonging.

Ephesians 2:12 reminds us of what life is like without reconciliation to God. The opposite of reconciliation is estrangement – not living as one. The apostle Paul reminds us – "…You were separate from Christ…excluded from citizenship *(belonging)*…foreigners to God's promises… without hope and without God in the world."

Being reconciled to Christ, we are no longer lost or separate, but found – and now living *In Christ*. We are included in His family, His inheritance, and His Kingdom.

We are no longer foreigners, but His dearly loved children experiencing the blessings promised in His Word. Reconciled to God, you can have a hope, a future – where God is with you and in you, in every situation.

The Road of Reconciliation leads to peace with God – and God's peace within us.

Ephesians 2:14-16 reminds us that *Jesus himself is our peace*. Without Jesus in our life, we will never experience true peace, and we will strive and try all sorts of ways and means to try and find peace.

Ephesians 2:17 – "Jesus came and preached peace to you who were far away and peace to those who were near."

Without reconciliation to Jesus (which comes by receiving Him as LORD of our lives) we will continue to carry around the heavy burden of the guilt and shame that accompanies our sinfulness.

The Road of Reconciliation will cause us to rejoice.

Romans 5:11 – "...we also rejoice in God, through our Lord Jesus Christ, through whom we have now received reconciliation."

Salvation, forgiveness, reconciliation, and eternal life... are all from God. As sinners, we open our hands and receive His grace and mercy that He pours towards us. Rejoice!

We need to remind ourselves that *the Gospel is not to make God acceptable to man – but to make man acceptable to God*. God made reconciliation possible in sending Jesus to the world. Again, I say Rejoice!

The Road of Reconciliation leads you into friendship with God.

For me personally, one of the greatest privileges of being a Christian is that God calls me His friend, and that can only be because Jesus paid the price (His life for my sin) – to reconcile me to God.

This day, God's hands of reconciliation reach out to you afresh, and He says "Come to me – be one with me – *I want to be your Friend*."

John 15:15 – "I no longer call you servants, because a servant does not know his master's business. Instead, I have called you friends, for everything that I learned from my Father I have made known to you."

The Road of Reconciliation draws us nearer to God.

God wants us to draw close to Him. "Come near!" Sci-Fi films talk of close encounters. How we need more close encounters with the power of the Living God.

Some years ago, on a Church weekend away, I recall seeing a long line of tall electricity pylons carrying large power cables across the landscape. It reminded me of the need to *'pray for the visible power of God to be evident within our individual lives, and in the Church – through the power of the Holy Spirit.'*

Closeness to God means that we will develop an intimate and authentic personal relationship with Him. In reconciling us to Himself, God wants us to experience His transforming power – where we come through changed.

I recall a request in a London City Mission prayer guide to pray for a man who had lost his faith due to events in his life. It read, *"Pray that God will draw him close."*

In times of trouble and adversity, as we walk towards God – He will be running towards us to meet and embrace us. We come with open hands – God comes with open arms.

The Road of Reconciliation calls us to be reconciled to God and one another.

It is great to know that we are reconciled to God – to experience His peace, knowing we are in right relationship with the Lord, because of His love for us and forgiveness offered. God is also calling each of us as His followers – to be reconciled to each other.

2 Corinthians 5:17-19 says – "Therefore if anyone is in Christ, he is a new creation; the old has gone, the new has come. All this is from God, who reconciled us to himself through Christ and gave us the ministry of reconciliation: that God was reconciling the world to himself, not counting men's sins against them. And He has committed to us the message of reconciliation."

We share the message of reconciliation when we share our testimony (as in Acts 4:20) – "As for us, there's no question – we can't keep quiet about what we've seen and heard." (The Message Bible)

As disciples of Jesus, we are all witnesses to *'Love's greatest story' – and* are called to share it with others. This was a title of an Easter song I wrote to share about the greatest news anyone could ever receive – that 'Jesus died for our sins to reconcile us back to God.'

"And it's Love's greatest story, that the King of all the world should die for me – and He rose from death in glory – turned the darkness and the pain to victory."

2 Corinthians 5:20 – "We are therefore Christ's ambassadors, as though God were making His appeal through us – we implore you on Christ's behalf: Be reconciled to God."

Jesus said in His Sermon on the Mount – that if you are offering gifts on the altar and there remember that your brother has something against you, leave the gift ... and *first go and be reconciled to your brother, then come and offer your gifts.*

Luke 12:58 – "As you are going with your adversary to the magistrate, try hard to be reconciled to him on the way..."

How are we doing in our peace-making and reconciling?

Friendship, remaining reconciled, and fellowship continues and grows where there is relationship, open communication, and commitment. These things need to be evident in our walk with God and our walk with one another.

Colossians 1:22-23 – "Now He has reconciled you by Christ's physical body through death to present you holy in His sight, without blemish and free from accusation – if you continue in your faith, established and firm, not moved from the hope held out in the gospel."

Reflection for prayer and action.

If you have not taken steps to be reconciled to God or are uncertain of being in right-relationship with God, use the prayer below as a guideline to receive Jesus Christ as your Lord, Saviour, and Friend.

"Lord Jesus Christ, I confess that I am a sinner. I have fallen short of your glory in my thinking, speaking and actions. Thank you, that you died on the Cross to forgive me of all my sin. I repent of my sinfulness, and I turn to follow You.

I receive your love and forgiveness and ask that You will help me live for You – and follow You – every day of my life. Come Holy Spirit to help, guide and strengthen me. I ask this in the Name of Jesus. Amen."

If you have prayed this prayer for the first time, from your heart – you have started your walk as a disciple of Jesus – and that journey continues for every day of your life as you obey and put into practice what God says in His Word. You are a child of God. "The Spirit himself testifies with our spirit that we are God's children." (Romans 8:16)

As God's children we will experience 'new life' – living in God's favour. 'Abundant life' – through God's Spirit within us, and 'eternal life' with Jesus in heaven – for our future hope.

The Drive of Discipleship

(The cost of being a disciple)

Readings – Luke 14:25-35 /
Matthew 28:16-20 (The Great Commission)

In Matthew 28:19-20 Jesus spoke these words. "*Therefore, go and make disciples of all nations,* baptising them in the name of the Father and of the Son and of the Holy Spirit, and teaching them to obey everything I have commanded you. And surely, I will be with you always, to the very end of the age."

When we have commenced the journey of following Jesus, discipleship is the continued learning of becoming more like Him in every aspect of our lives – everyday.

The characteristics and qualities that we are to display as disciples of Jesus are many. Let us consider the topic of discipleship itself – looking at 3 main points.

1) The Call from Jesus to be His disciple.

2) The Cost of being a disciple.

3) The Commission to make disciples.

If we are disciples, we are to follow the example, words and teaching of Jesus Christ.

We have committed ourselves to Him – walking Christ's way, living Christ's life, and sharing His love and truth with others.

In following Jesus, we are to be learners. Learning by listening, watching, and imitating. This is what Jesus meant in Matthew 11:29 when He said, "*Take my yoke upon you and learn from me,* for I am gentle and humble in heart, and you will find rest for your souls."

The heart of being a disciple is to harness up to Jesus' yoke. That way, we will remain close to Him.

Let us look at how Jesus trained and taught His disciples.

In Acts 1:1 – Luke says, "In my former book, I wrote about all that Jesus began to do and to teach, until the day He was taken up to heaven..." In the gospels, we read and observe how Jesus taught by His actions and His words.

At the College where I used to work, there was a poster over each mirror in the Staff toilets. It was a quote by Benjamin Franklin which read, "Tell me and I forget, teach me and I may remember, involve me and I learn."

This is how Jesus trained His disciples; by involving them.

Jesus called His disciples to be with Him. He gave them an example. They watched Him work and they worked with Him, and very importantly – they asked Jesus questions, especially when they failed.

Jesus sent them out in pairs to practice what they had learnt. They reported back – asked more questions – and received further instructions.

It can be very beneficial in our corporate prayer meetings

(and worship meetings) to ask God a question; – pause and wait for several minutes, and then speak out what God has brought to our heart and mind during that quiet time.

Although Jesus spoke to multitudes, most of His discipling and teaching was accomplished when meeting people one to one, in twos and threes or with His disciples. Making disciples came from people living, working, and sharing together in small groups.

This commitment 'in Christ' to one another,
is also part of the cost of being a disciple.

Jesus often shared about the cost of following Him. He outlined what being a disciple would involve, and many turned away. More than five hundred saw the risen Christ, but only one hundred and twenty were waiting in the upper room for the promise of the Holy Spirit. Those 120 – were willing to accept His call.

In Luke 14:25-33 Jesus shares some hard-hitting truths concerning the cost of being a disciple. He said, "If anyone comes to me and does not hate his father and mother, his wife and children, his brothers and sisters – yes even his own life – he cannot be my disciple."

This does not mean we are to hate our family and ourselves, but rather, our love for Jesus must be so great that, in comparison, our love for others and self will seem like hate. Jesus taught that the *most important commandment* is to love God with all your heart … and the second is to love your neighbour as yourself. (See Mark 12:28-31) We are to make our relationship of loving, following, and serving Jesus – our top priority.

This is what the Lordship of Jesus means. As the old saying goes – "If Jesus is not LORD of ALL, He is not LORD at all."

Just as we are told in the 10 commandments that God is a jealous God – that we are not to make ourselves idols, nor bow down and worship them, we need to ensure there is nothing taking equal claim to our loyalty, commitment, and devotion to Jesus.

Jesus is both LORD and KING. His Word has authority and we need to obey what He asks and says.

In Luke 14:27 – Jesus said "...anyone who does not carry his cross and follow me cannot be my disciple."

Galatians 2:20 reminds us – "I have been crucified with Christ, and I no longer live, but Christ lives in me. The life I live in the body I live by faith in the Son of God, who loved me and gave himself for me."

We may be familiar with the verse, but it would be wise to consider afresh what being dead to self and crucified with Christ means.

We are dead to what we would selfishly want to do and we choose to follow Jesus in every situation – whatever the cost. Like Jesus, we are to lay down our will and desires and follow the will of God.

Jesus is looking for finishers. Like the person building a tower, they must consider the cost. Discipleship is a call of uncompromising obedience – *once we start – there is no stopping and no turning back.*

The second illustration Jesus gives, is one of a King going to war. Before he attacks, he must count his own soldiers and the enemy's soldiers. As Christ's disciples we enter into spiritual warfare daily. From the moment you awake each morning, there is a battle raging for your allegiance.

Your old nature, and anything else Satan may try to use will try to lead you back into sin, temptation, and failure.

Jesus never said the Christian life was an easy one. Be ready for a battle!

Jesus concludes this passage by adding "In the same way, any of you who does not give up everything he has cannot be my disciple."

In our day and culture, we must not make any less of these commands. God in His great love, longs for what is best for us. Total obedience and faith in God are two key discipleship issues that will keep us walking close to the Lord.

Knowing how much we are loved and forgiven keeps us pressing on. God's amazing grace (His favour and His Holy Spirit's enabling presence) will always be sufficient for every need – in joy and sorrow – giving us hope to endure and to finish life well.

Let us look at Jesus' commission to go and make disciples.

There is great rejoicing in heaven when a person is saved

(becomes a Christian) Sometimes we may see radical changes in people the moment they become believers through the power of God working in their lives.

Whatever our conversion experience we will all have continuing issues of discipleship to work through every day of our lives.

Evangelists have a specific gifting to bring people to Christ, but I personally believe that we all have a responsibility and ability to make disciples.

Colossians 1:28 reveals another aim in discipleship. "*We proclaim Him, admonishing and teaching everyone with all wisdom, so that we present everyone perfect (mature) in Christ.*"

Being a disciple and follower of Jesus Christ will affect our relationships at home, in our work-place and at Church, and also our attitudes and behaviour, so it is evident to those around us that we are becoming more Christ-like.

The challenge and call to discipleship – covers every aspect of our lives.

As a Church (corporate) we need to commit to discipling one another – spurring each other on, and using our gifts to minister God's grace to each other.

Hebrews 10:24-25 instructs us – "We should *keep on encouraging each other to be thoughtful and to do helpful things.* Some people have given up the habit of meeting for worship, but we must not do that. We should keep on encouraging each other, especially since you know that the day of the Lord's coming is getting closer."

Making disciples today is making the next generation of preachers and teachers of God's Word – the next generation of Church Leaders, Pastors, Missionaries and Prayer Intercessors .... Only discipleship can produce 'fruitful spiritual ministries.'

I have shared this many times in my preaching; that the high calling and great purpose in discipleship and Christian living, is *to increase in our love for Jesus*. This will always be my personal aim as a disciple. *'To love Jesus more and to have more of Him in my life.'* Love will always be the greatest and love will always be the most excellent way. Love never fails! (See 1 Corinthians 13)

Being a disciple of Jesus means we are:

willing to serve / learning to listen / willing to learn / willing to be corrected / able to submit to God and one another / sharing our lives with others / learning humility / examining our own life and motives /able to forgive / to be trusted / minding our own business / faithful in the small things / aiming to put God first in all aspects of our life /quick to obey when God speaks, corrects and convicts / putting our faith and trust in God for everything.

May the LORD enable each of us to make disciples and bring believers to maturity in Jesus Christ.

Reflection for prayer and action.

- Am I remaining teachable in every aspect of my life? Am I open to be corrected and guided by fellow believers?
- Is my love for Jesus increasing as the weeks pass by? Is there any area in my walk as a disciple of Jesus, where my heart may have become hardened or my love for Him has become cold?
- Take time to pray and consider the aspect of prayer partners, or small – prayer support groups. The specific purpose of these, is to offer help to one another in your daily life as a disciple – to give encouragement, accountability, and a listening ear, and praying into any problems or challenges that we face – so that we enable and encourage each other to be the people that Jesus wants us to be.
- Think of those people or groups over the years that have helped and encouraged you in your walk with Jesus. Give praise to God for them, and pray about who you may be able to mentor or support in some way – on their journey of discipleship.

The Pathway of Praise

Reading – Psalm 138

King David wrote many psalms of praise to God. It is good to take time to worship and give thanks to the LORD before we ask of Him in prayer. David proclaimed, "I will exalt you, my God the King; I will praise your name for ever and ever. Every day I will praise you and extol your name for ever and ever. Great is the LORD and most worthy of praise..." (Psalm 145:1-3a)

In what ways can we bring praise to God?

1) *Accepting one another* – Romans 15:7: "Accept one another, then, just as Christ accepted you, in order to bring praise to God."
2) Hebrews 13:15 – "Through Jesus Christ, therefore, let us *continually offer to God a sacrifice of praise – the fruit of our lips that confess His name.*"
3) *When we are happy*. James 5:13 – "Is anyone happy? Let him sing songs of praise."

In Jesus Christ we were chosen.... (Ephesians 1:11-12) – in order that we ...might be for the praise of His glory.

The pathway of praise broadens as we walk it.

- Psalm 71:14 – "But as for me I shall always have hope; *I will praise You more and more.*"

- Psalm 119:175 – "*Let me live that I may praise You,...*"
- Psalm 79:13 – "Then we your people, the sheep of your pasture, will *praise you forever; from generation to generation we will recount your praise.*"
- Psalm 147:1 "Praise the Lord. (Hallelujah) *How good it is to sing praises to our God, how pleasant and fitting to praise Him!*"

We should encourage and teach one another how to pray – and in addition, how to praise.

The pathway of praise is a path we choose to walk on.

The opening sentence of verse 1 of Psalm 138 – reveals that we need to choose to praise and worship God – full heartedly. "I will praise you, O LORD with all my heart."

Our praise, worship, and thankfulness that we offer to God must be authentic and sincere.

Mighty victories have been accomplished – and strongholds broken, through the power of praise to the Lord.

In Acts 16:25-26 – As Paul and Silas were praying and singing hymns to God (in prison) – an earthquake shook the foundations of the prison and all the doors flew open.

Joshua's people gave a shout! (See Joshua 6:20) The wall of the city collapsed, and they went in to take the city. We are not told exactly what the shout was – but *shouts to God in praise are powerful!*

Psalm 35:27 "May those who delight in my vindication (meaning you are justified in God-made righteous) *shout for joy and gladness; may they always say – The LORD be exalted."*

Psalm 95:1 – Come, let us sing for joy to the LORD, let us shout aloud to the Rock of our salvation.

These verses underline the importance of audible praise and thanksgiving. In my late teens I visited a Church in South Chard, Somerset. It was here, that I first experienced the joy and blessing of offering my devotion and worship to the Lord out loud – along with others at the same time. David declared in his psalm, "My mouth is filled with your praise, declaring your splendour all day long." (Psalm 70:8)

The pathway of praise is a single track.

Our praise and worship is to the Lord Jesus Christ alone – who is the Only Way to our Father God. v1b declares, "Before the gods I will sing your praise." (v2) We need to ensure that God gets all the praise, honour, and glory.

Worship is all about God captivating our hearts. Daily discipleship of prayer and reading God's word keeps us on the path. Have we any gods that remain, or have crept back into our lives that are preventing us from worshipping and praising the LORD as we should?

The pathway of praise requires us to use our minds and our bodies in thanksgiving.

David in this Psalm chose to bow down towards God's holy temple.

There are many other physical expressions we can offer to God as our sacrifice of praise. Playing musical instruments, clapping, dancing, kneeling, laying prostrate, marching, raising hands, singing, standing, waving…

Even when our circumstances are difficult and we may find it hard to give thanks to the Lord in all situations – we are still commanded to do this, for it is God's will for us in Christ Jesus. (See 1 Thessalonians 5:18)

"This is the way God wants you who belong to Christ Jesus to live." (The Message Bible)

To enable us, God's Word gives us many reasons to be thankful. Why not make a list of your own personal reasons to give thanks as you remember God's goodness and faithfulness to you over the years?

The pathway of praise discovers and acknowledges God's blessing and grace.

I will praise your name for your love and faithfulness. (v2)

I will praise your name for you have exalted above all things your name and your word.

I will praise You – for when I call, You answer me. (v3) This is where we see prayer and praise walking hand in hand – with our knowledge and understanding about God from reading scripture.

I will praise You – because You have made me bold and stout hearted. (v3)

Verse 4 expresses a prayer about praise. "May all the kings

of the earth praise you, O Lord when they hear the words of your mouth." In these words, we see that God is King of Kings. He is Sovereign over every other King and authority, and David's prayer is that kings of the earth will praise the King of Heaven and Earth.

We can also use the word 'may' as a blessing or prophetic proclamation – as an assurance – not a possibility. *"May you know God's peace, presence and grace."*

'May they (kings) sing of the ways of the Lord, for the glory of the Lord is great.' May we also *sing of the ways of the Lord* because of His great glory.

What are the ways of the Lord? Love – peace – joy – forgiveness – righteousness – justice – mercy – truth – compassion – holiness...

I will praise you Lord, for although You are on high, You look upon the lowly. I will praise You Lord – although I walk in the midst of trouble you preserve my life ... your right hand saves me.

In verse 8 – We can praise God for He will fulfil His purposes for us and in us, for His love endures forever. The closing words change to a prayer. "Do not abandon the works of your hands." We can make that our prayer and turn it into praise as we acknowledge God's promise. *"Thank you Lord, that you do not abandon the works of your hands."*

May we choose to walk the pathway of praise and thanksgiving daily, and when we meet to worship together as disciples of Jesus.

Reflection for prayer and action.

- Build praise and thanksgiving to God into your daily life and routines.
- Write your own song or verse of praise to the Lord. Thank Him for who He is, in addition to all that He does. Express your appreciation for all that Jesus means to you. Acknowledge all the daily blessings He bestows on you.
- In your prayers of asking and intercession – add your praise and worship – thanking God for His Word and promises, His faithfulness and goodness.
- We can pray audibly or quietly. Our praise and thankfulness to the LORD has great power when expressed aloud, either when we are alone or worshipping with others. (Our worship becomes a witness – to God's goodness and greatness) Psalm 66:8 encourages us to, "Praise our God, O peoples, let the sound of His praise be heard." Take some time to praise God 'out loud' this week.

The Place of Prayer

8 aspects of prayer (Lord teach us to pray)

Reading – Luke 11:1-13

A key principle for Discipleship issues is always to keep learning and stay teachable. Prayer – our access to God, must be a continuing journey of learning, practice, and review. I would like to share with you 8 key scriptural aspects about prayer that I have personally found helpful.

Prayer is being real before God.

Whatever circumstances you are experiencing – you can pour out your heart to God. It took me a long time in my Christian life to realise that it was reasonable to offload onto the LORD. (King David would say "I am restless with my complaint.")

I love Psalm 139, which speaks of how closely God knows, sees, and understands us. There is nowhere we can go, where His Spirit is not present. David acknowledges that God's thoughts to him are precious – and if he counted them, they would outnumber the grains of sand on the sea-shore. We also are in God's thoughts. You, are on His mind right now.

Suddenly the prayer changes in verse 19, "If only you would slay the wicked O God! Away from me, you bloodthirsty men! They speak of you with evil intent; your adversaries misuse your name. Do I not hate those who hate you O Lord, and abhor those who rise up against You? I have nothing but hatred for them, I count them my enemies."

That is being real before God.

David was also very direct in his prayers. He had been betrayed and says to God (Psalm 55:1-2a) "Listen to my prayer, O God, do not ignore my plea; hear me and answer me. My thoughts trouble me and I am distraught." That is authentic prayer, honest, desperate, truthful – and from the heart.

We need to practice prayer.

We live in a culture (especially in the business world) where we aim to deliver excellence without error or mistakes. That is a good goal. However, being human means, we will get things wrong.

For Christians also – as we desire to give our best to God, and be our best for God, we will still fall short many times as we learn.

When it comes to spiritual ministries within the Church, (prayer being one of the main ones) we need to have an openness and acceptance as we learn and practice prayer corporately.

One of Jesus' disciples asked Him, "Lord teach us to pray, just as John taught his disciples." (Luke 11:1)

Extemporary, spontaneous prayer (without preparation – from the heart) is not always going to be word perfect. Like most of us, I have made some blunders in extemporary prayer. (and I still make a few)

How many of us are still held back from praying publicly, being anxious about how our prayers may come across to others?

Our great assurance is this. Jesus is praying for you right now. “He is at the right hand of God and is also interceding for us.” (See Romans 8:34)

He sees and knows our hearts – especially in those times when our words seem inadequate.

If Church congregations had not allowed, or encouraged me to preach to them before my theology was deeper, I may not have progressed to the privilege of regular preaching as I do today.

Any area in spiritual ministry, including praying for, receiving and exercising spiritual gifts – praying for the sick or other needs – discerning the guidance of God – developing song worship within Church congregations – *all takes time – and practice.*

Any new step of faith and direction means that we will move into new territory, which is the usual ground for making more mistakes, while we are learning and being taught.

As disciples of Jesus, our faith and trust is in Him. The writer of Proverbs reminds us to, “Trust GOD from the bottom of your heart; don’t try to figure out everything on your own. Listen for God’s voice in everything you do, everywhere you go; He’s the one who will keep you on track.” (Proverbs 3:5-6 – The Message Bible)

We need to be consistent and persistent in our praying.

In Luke 18:1-8 (The parable of the Persistent Widow). Jesus told His disciples a parable to show them they should always pray and not give up. The widow kept asking the judge for justice against her adversary.

v7 – “Will not God bring about justice for His chosen ones, who cry out to him day and night?”

When we bring to the Lord our intercessory prayers for a person or a situation – we need to sense what the Holy Spirit is calling us to do.

Our prayer for some may be a one off, where we ask God to bless them ‘today’ or we may be led to pray for a person daily through a certain season of their lives.

When I am specifically praying for healing for people – I’m constantly drawn to Jesus’ words in Luke 11:9-10.

“Ask and it will be given to you; seek and you will find; knock and the door will be opened to you. For everyone who asks receives; he who seeks finds; and to him who knocks, the door will be opened.”

I believe with all my heart that every time we pray, God always does something. It may not be what we ask – or in our time scale – but God always hears our prayers and responds.

God is always working on bringing wholeness to our lives – using every situation we go through to teach us something and to make us more like Jesus – as we trust Him.

Prayer is more about hearing
from God than asking of God.

Psalm 5:3 reminds us, "...morning by morning *I lay my requests before You and wait in expectation*."

Isaiah 64:4 – "Since ancient times no-one has heard ... no ear has perceived ... *no eye has seen any God besides You, who acts on behalf of those who wait for Him.*"

The heart and centre of fellowship with the Holy Spirit and growing in God, is that God wants to hear from us, and He wants to talk to us.

So often in our praying, we make our requests and we do not give God time to speak to us. As we wait on the Lord in prayer (individually and corporately as a Church) we will experience how the Holy Spirit brings scriptures to our remembrance, a word – or a picture illustration to our mind – that will encourage, comfort, or guide us.

Be specific in our prayer requests.

In Mark 10:46-52 we read about blind Bartimaeus calling out to Jesus to have mercy on him. Jesus called Bartimaeus to Him and asks what may appear an obvious question to a blind person. "What do you want me to do for you?"

Bartimaeus was begging – he could have asked for money. Jesus asked the question because he wanted to draw out a heart response. "Rabbi – I want to see."

"Go," Jesus said, "Your faith has healed you." Immediately he received his sight. What do you want Jesus to do for you? May the Lord encourage us to pray boldly and specifically for ourselves and the needs of others – in His Name and for His glory.

Offer prayers of faith.

James 5:14-15 poses the question, "Is any one of you sick. He should call the elders of the Church to pray over him and anoint him with oil in the Name of the Lord. And the prayer offered in faith will make the sick person well; the Lord will raise him up."

On each double page of my prayer journal, I write to remind myself, "What impossible things am I praying for?" – for we serve God with whom all things are possible. Nothing is too difficult for the LORD.

Philippians 4:6 tells us "Do not be anxious about anything, but in everything, by prayer and petition, with thanksgiving, present your request to God."

We often forget to pray with thanksgiving.

We could pray the following for a person in need of healing – adding in our thanksgiving. "Lord, I bring ... (name of person) to You, and *I thank You that You are the LORD who forgives sin and heals diseases*. I ask that You will touch them please with your healing love – restoring their health – making them whole. *Thank You Lord, that You are the Life Giver*. May they know a fresh touch of your resurrection life in their body. *Praise you Lord Jesus for hearing my prayer. All glory and honour be to your Name*. Amen."

Our prayers of faith, are in God's faithfulness to watch over and perform His word in our lives.

Finally – Pray from Heavens perspective.

I know that the Coming Kingdom of God, is a going to be a physical Kingdom when Jesus comes again to rule and reign on earth. But as spiritual believers, the Kingdom of God is a spiritual reality NOW.

Although we see some glimpses of heaven on earth now, we need to see more. Sometimes in our requests to God we put a full stop after praying, 'Your kingdom come, your will be done.' Praying from Heaven's perspective says – *'Your will be done on earth as it is in heaven.'*

Ephesians 3:20 (The Message Bible) declares, "God can do anything you know – far more than you could ever imagine or guess or request in your wildest dreams! He does it not by pushing us around but by working within us, His Spirit deeply and gently within us."

This chapter has only just touched the surface on aspects of prayer and what it is to seek God and to hear from Him. There will always be so much more...

May each of us continue to ask, "Lord teach us to pray." – and then we need to share with each other what He teaches us.

Reflection for prayer and action.

- Like the disciples of Jesus, ask – "LORD, please teach me to pray."
- Am I taking time to listen to Jesus – to hear His voice, or are my prayers more about asking for things for others or myself?
- How could I make prayer and seeking the Lord my top priority?
- Is there a person or situation that the LORD may be calling you to pray for on a daily or regular basis – or for a specific season? This may be for them to come to know Jesus as Saviour, for healing, provision, or guidance.
- If you do not already, try keeping a Prayer Journal. Use it in a way that will help you best in your praying. Write down those scriptures that encourage you to pray and the lessons you are learning on your devotional journey. Listing people and situations you are praying for, makes a good reminder to 'be persistent in prayer.' Give thanks and praise to the LORD in the waiting times and when He answers your prayers.

5

The Trunk Road of Truth

Reading – John 8:12-47

The chapters in this book, high-light various roads linked with themes – to underline that discipleship is a journey, a road we walk, a pathway we tread. We are to keep walking consistently, and faithfully with perseverance – every day of our lives that God grants to us – or until Jesus returns.

Why the 'Trunk Road of Truth'? By definition, a trunk road is an important main road used for long-distance travel. It can remind us that on our life-long journey of discipleship – to heed biblical truth is essential – in enabling us to become more like Jesus and live a life that brings glory to Him.

As we consider this theme of truth – let us look at the following aspects. The God of all Truth; truth, from the perspective of being honest with ourselves and others and the truth of God's Word – that sets us free!

God of all truth.

In John 18:33 we read about Pilate asking Jesus, "Are you the King of the Jews?"

Later, Jesus answered, "You are right in saying I am a King. In fact, for this reason I was born, and for this I came into the world, to testify to the truth. *Everyone on the side of truth listens to me.*" To which Pilate questions – "What is Truth?" (John 18:38)

This is still one of the biggest questions of today. "What is truth?" and when it comes to our personal faith and trust in God – "Who is truth?"

Jesus says these amazing words in John 14:6. They are strong foundation words of truth, which set the Christian faith apart from any other faith or religion.

Jesus said (in context of guiding the way to the eternal heavenly dwelling which He has prepared for us) – *"I am the Way and The Truth and the Life. No-one comes to the Father except through me."*

King David the Psalmist prayed to God asking "...guide me in your truth and teach me ..." (Psalm 25:5a) He knew that God's Word and will was 'The truth' – that would reveal God's heart and purposes, guide him, and give him hope every day. Later in Psalm 31:5 he says "...redeem me, O Lord, the God of Truth."

Time and time again in the New Testament, Jesus starts His teaching with the words – "I tell you the truth..."

It is not because he wants us to know He isn't lying, but wants to underline and constantly bring to our remembrance and attention, things that are true – that are worth living our lives for – that will give us a hope and a future, keep us from brokenness and sinfulness and lead and keep us in right relationship with God and others.

Be true to God, true to others
and true to ourselves.

When I was young in my Christian faith, I recall a comment made to me by a girl – who told me 'I was too honest.' The emphasis being on the word 'too.' The truth is, we are either honest or dishonest. The word 'too' can mean to a higher degree than desirable.

Psalm 51:6 instructs us, "Surely you desire truth in the inner parts" – our innermost being – in our personal thinking – from the heart. The Message Bible puts it like this. "What you're after is truth from the inside out…"

I am sure we've all had those times when our honesty (acting and speaking truly) has been noted and appreciated – like telling the person at the check-out till they have given you too much change or confessing to someone about damage done to their property – when you could have got away with it.

I recall telling a shop assistant about damage I had done on a book cover while browsing. She replied, "No problem, your conscience is clear!"

The apostle Paul states in Acts 24:16, "So I strive to keep my conscience clear before God and man." Being truthful could cost us money – but God will always honour it.

Like with any good habit we want to establish – you have to practice it and build principles into your life that will help you.

I used to work at a Holiday Farm Complex, and if I found any small coins while working or cleaning – I would give them to my employer. It may be pennies, 50p or £1 coins. One day, I found a £50 note under a hedge in the car park area. It was no more difficult passing that 'big note' back, as I had the principle firmly established in me.

Any time we are aware that we have not acted or spoken in truth (including those occasions when exaggeration creeps into our conversation) – we need to keep short accounts with the Lord. Ask for His forgiveness and His continued help – to enable you to 'walk in the truth.'

King David the psalmist said, "Your love is ever before me, and I walk continually in your truth." (Psalm 26:3)

Seeking and sharing God's truth and acting and speaking in truth – comes from our love for God and desire to please Him.

Receiving afresh, and praising God for His amazing love, forgiveness, undeserved favour, and mercy towards us – is always a strength, help, and way forward – as we desire to live and speak God's truth.

Living and declaring the truth is vital to Christian maturity – to becoming like our Saviour Jesus. "Truthful witness by a good person clears the air, but liars lay down a smoke screen of deceit." (Proverbs 12:17 – The Message Bible)

Proverbs 12:22 goes on to remind us that when we are truthful – God delights in us!

Only the truth sets us truly free.

Let us underline the promise from Jesus in the passage we read. Jesus said, "If you hold to my teaching, you are really my disciples. Then *you will know the truth, and the truth will set you free.*" (John 8:31-32) Every time we 'read and heed' what God asks of us in His Word – we will experience more freedom.

Jesus went on to say, "If the Son sets you free, you will be free indeed!" (John 8:36)

Paul also reminds us of this truth in 2 Corinthians 3:17 – "The Lord is the Spirit, and where the Spirit of the Lord is, there is freedom." There will be liberty. The Lord's teachings are truth, and only His teachings will set us free.

Relative truth declares that something is true for one person and not to another. What God says in His Word (the Bible) is 'absolute truth' – for all people. Isaiah the prophet warned about the relative truth mindset that we are seeing in our time and the consequences of turning aside from God's Word of absolute truth.

Isaiah said, "Woe to those who call evil good and good evil, who put darkness for light and light for darkness, who put bitter for sweet and sweet for bitter. Woe to those who are wise in their own eyes and clever in their own sight." (Isaiah 5:20-21)

God is calling His people to stand firm in these days as we live out and proclaim the truth of His word.

The scripture verse we so often quote (Ephesians 4:15) – "Instead, speaking the truth in love" – was set in the context of God equipping and preparing His people for works of service – building them up in unity and faith – in the knowledge of the Son of God – into maturity and the fullness of Christ.

Paul reminds us when we speak the truth in love; we will in all things grow up into Him (Christ) who is the Head.

This is where we need to seek and ask for Holy Spirit strength, wisdom, and power – to share God's truth, and it is out of our love for people that we want to see them set free by the absolute truth of what God says through His Word. The psalmist proclaimed (Psalm 119:160) "All your words are true; all your righteous laws are eternal."

We can pray – "Lord Jesus, please give me the courage, but also the love I need towards others – to share the truth with them."

Reflection for prayer and action.

- Give thanks to God that He is the God of all truth. He is true to His word and character in all things.
- What principles have I learnt and built into my life to help me remain truthful in my thoughts, words, and actions?
- Do I need to ask Jesus' forgiveness for any aspect in my life where I have not spoken the truth, or not acted truthfully?
- Is there any aspect of God's Word, where I am tempted to compromise the truth of what He says – because I risk not being accepted, challenged, or seen as narrow minded by other people? The psalmist wrote and prayed concerning his love for God's statutes – *"Don't ever deprive me of truth, not ever – your commandments are what I depend on. Oh, I'll guard with my life what you've revealed to me, guard it now, guard it ever…"* (Psalm 119:43-44 –The Message Bible) Ask the LORD to help you remain strong in living out and speaking His Word of truth to others.

6

The Ridge of Right Relationship

Readings – 1 John 1:5-2:6 / Romans 12:9-21

As we continue our walk of discipleship let us take a trek along the Ridge of 'Right Relationship' – looking at what it means to live daily in right relationship with God and with one another.

This builds on the message of the first chapter, where we looked at 'The road of reconciliation.'

I read a quote from a keen walker who said, "One of the greatest joys in the life of a backpacker is to walk along a ridge line. That line marks the very top of the mountains where you can climb no more and you get to enjoy the thousands of feet of space below."

Maybe there is a parallel here, where our highest purpose in our walk of discipleship – is to reach that place of intimacy with God – where we can enjoy just being in His presence, and sharing fellowship with Him, knowing that we are His friends.

We often hear the saying that Christianity is not about religion. It is a relationship – a personal and authentic friendship with God.

Religion sees men and women trying to reach out to God. Christianity is about Christ reaching down and coming to us.

Jesus, the Living Word; became flesh and lived for a while among us, teaching that we could know friendship with God now and for eternity.

The 10 commandments are all about relationship. The first four are about our relationship with God, and the next six are about our relationship with others.

How do we come into right relationship with God?

Jesus came to be the Saviour of the world. We are all sinners and fall short of the glory of God. 1 John 1:9 reminds us that, "If we confess our sins, He is faithful and just and will forgive us our sins and purify us from all unrighteousness."

We receive God's forgiveness, and as we choose to repent (not just be sorry for our sinfulness but to turn our lives around) we will experience the power of the Holy Spirit within us – to enable us to live lives that are pleasing to God. 1 John 2:9 reads, "We know that we have come to know Him if we obey His commands."

Our Salvation cost Jesus His life. He shed His blood on the Cross, paying the price for our sins so that we could live in right relationship with God.

When we receive Christ, we become His disciples – we side with Him, and day by day we choose to follow the ways of Jesus rather than walk our own path in life.

The main aspect of daily discipleship (as John explains) is "Walking in the light." God is light – in Him there is no darkness at all." (1 John 1:5)

Right relationship with God is about remaining in fellowship with Him as we walk in the light and in obedience to His Word.

The key aspects of our right relationship with God are:

Knowing we are loved by God – and we are to love Him with all our heart, soul, mind, and strength.

Receiving God's forgiveness in Jesus.

Our trust and obedience to God and how we fellowship (communicate) with Him.

Communication is vital in any relationship.

Relationships break down when people don't communicate or listen to others. We need to talk with God and listen for His voice.

As we pray and read the Bible – we will hear the Holy Spirit's words of counsel, guidance, and teaching.

When we wait on the Lord – we can be open to receive an impression, picture, or scripture that He brings to our remembrance to encourage us in our walk with Him.

Each time we skip a prayer or bible reading time, we miss out on an opportunity of deepening, strengthening, and maintaining our relationship with the LORD.

In Psalm 51:10-12 – when King David had really messed up by committing adultery and murder – he prayed this amazing prayer. "Create in me a clean heart O God, and renew a right spirit within me. Cast me not away from your presence, and take not your Holy Spirit from me. Restore to me the joy of your salvation, and uphold me with a willing spirit."

This is the prayer to pray when we need to get back into right relationship with God. David had sinned against God and trespassed against others.

These key aspects of love, forgiveness, maintaining right relationship with God, is what we must work out in our lives with our friends, family, church fellowship, work colleagues, our critics, cynics and even enemies.

God gives of himself to us completely – in abundance. The Spirit of God wants to fill us with His fruit and the characteristics of Jesus – so they can overflow from us – touching the lives of other people.

The work of the Spirit of God in us will enable us to "Love our enemies and pray for those who persecute us." (Matthew 5:44)

Each time someone offends us or sins against us – we need to turn to the Cross of Christ and see the love and forgiveness of Jesus poured out for us.

It is in understanding God's love and forgiveness towards us – that will enable us to forgive a person 490 times – and after that ... again and again (See Matthew 18:22) This is the right relationship of mercy – as God has shown towards us.

We must let people go – release them – leave them at the foot of the Cross, where we all find love, mercy, forgiveness, and reconciliation with God and one another.

The heart and core of discipleship is loving God and loving others. Our powerful witness for Jesus to a dark and lost world – is to love people as He loves us.

Jesus said, "A new commandment I give to you, that you love one another: just as I have loved you, you also are to love one another. By this all people will know that you are my disciples, if you have love for one another." (John 13:34-35)

As we work towards right relationship with God first – right relationship with others will follow. It may sound simplistic – but the answer is always "MORE OF GOD – less of me."

John the Baptist declared of Christ, "He must become greater; I must become less." (John 3:30) The Message Bible reads – 'This is the assigned moment for Him to move into the centre, while I slip off to the sidelines.'

Let us look at a few areas where we can deepen our relationship with God and each other.

In our friendship, fellowship and communication with God and others we need to be real. Be yourself.

We may be able to hide things from others, but God is all knowing. There is no mask that we can wear that God does not see through.

As a young believer, when I attended our youth group meetings, I tried to impart only the positive things about my Christian experience, because my motive was to inspire and encourage them.

However; after a time, when I felt I could share about my

struggles and failures – others would also open up about similar challenges they faced – and we realised we were not alone in our difficulties and we could then talk about the issues and support one another.

The place of fellowship and meaningful relationship with each other means we can admit our weaknesses. It takes humility.

Peter said, "Clothe yourselves, all of you with humility toward one another, for God opposes the proud but gives grace to the humble. Humble yourselves, therefore under the mighty hand of God..." (1 Peter 5:5b-6a)

Being real, means the Church needs to be the place where we can share our true feelings about our concerns and struggles and know we will still be loved, accepted, and supported.

In our relationship with others, we need to keep in mind, and practice the Mathew 18 principle.

"If your brother or sister sins, go and point out their fault, just between the two of you. If they listen to you, you have won them over. But *if they will not listen, take one or two others along, so that 'every matter may be established by the testimony of two or three witnesses.' If they still refuse to listen, tell it to the church;...*" (Matthew 18:15-18)

1 John 1:7 explains – "But if we walk in the light, as He is in the light, we have fellowship with one another..."

As we share life together – we will get to know each other better and understand we are a group of people, with hugely varied interests and preferences.

Therefore, as we come as one to love and serve God – He calls His people to *be courteous* as we *show respect for our differences – considerate of the feelings of others*.

Paul reminds us in Romans 15:2 – "Let each of us please his neighbour for his good, to build him up."

Titus said – "...avoid quarrelling, to be gentle, and to show perfect courtesy toward all people." (Titus 3:2)

Finally – walking the ridge of right relationship with each other thrives on encouragement – as we give and receive from one another.

Paul wrote in Romans 1:11-12 – "For I long to see you, that I may impart to you some spiritual gift to strengthen you – that is, that we may be mutually encouraged by each other's faith, both yours and mine."

Paul went on to say in Romans 14:19 – "So then let us pursue what makes for peace and for mutual upbuilding."

May each of us know the power and presence of God – to walk in right relationship with Him and one another.

Reflection for prayer and action.

- As on any long journey, take time to rest and reflect on where you have come from and where you are going in your walk with God. In some areas of our discipleship, we may not be where we want to be yet. (For example, I may be patient, but I could be more patient. I may be loving, but I can become more loving – In Christ)
- Is there anyone you sense that you are not in right relationship with? If someone has trespassed against you, it is vital to come to the place of 'forgiveness' as soon as possible. It may take the support and prayer of a fellow disciple and close friend – but seek to obey the words of Jesus in the prayer He taught His disciples saying – "Forgive us our sins, for *we also forgive everyone* who sins against us." (Luke 11:4a)
- Give thanks to Jesus for His amazing grace, love, and forgiveness towards you. Ask Him to fill you with His love and forgiveness towards others through the power of the Holy Spirit – who lives in you.

The Route of Integrity

Reading – 1 Chronicles 29:10-20 (David's Prayer)

As we continue our journey of discipleship, let us take a walk along the 'Route of Integrity.' Just like the writing that runs through a stick of candy rock, God desires integrity to be visible and readable, in and through every aspect of our lives.

King David had been speaking about key principles in scripture concerning giving and stewardship. To God, our reasons for 'why' we give are more important that 'what' we give. David stated in his prayer to the Lord, "Everything comes from You, and we have given You only what comes from your hand … I know my God, that You test the heart and are pleased with integrity. All these things have I given willingly and with honest intent." (1 Chronicles 29:14b, 17a)

Let us look at what Integrity is, and how it is made evident in three important areas of discipleship. *Accountability, Responsibility and Confidentiality.*

How do we define Integrity?

If we check with a dictionary, we will see it is about honesty, sincerity, fairness, righteousness – doing the right thing in a reliable way. It is like a compass that never wavers – it speaks of a wholeness and undivided heart and mind in our life principles. Integrity is more about who we are (especially when we are alone) than what we do.

What does the Bible say about the way of Integrity?

Proverbs 11:3 – "*The integrity of the upright guides them* – but the unfaithful are destroyed by their duplicity." (two-facedness)

Proverbs 13:6 – "*Righteousness guards the man of integrity*, but wickedness overthrows the sinner."

Psalm 119:1 (New Living Translation) – "*Joyful (blessed) are people of integrity,* who follow the instructions of the LORD."

God declared His servant Job to be a man of integrity. God spoke to Satan about Job saying – he is blameless, upright, a man who fears God and shuns evil, and he still maintains his integrity though you incited me against him – to ruin him without reason. (Job 2:3)

The plan of Satan – 'to ruin without reason'- reveals why Satan is a deceiver, liar, and thief. In contrast – God has created us for His purposes.

When Job lost his sons, daughters, cattle, and camels – his wife asked "*Are you still holding on to your integrity?*" (Job 2:9) A question we must ask of ourselves.

Integrity in accountability and responsibility are very closely linked. John Wesley (the 18th century Methodist leader) established 'Accountability Discipleship Groups.' These were small, covenant discipleship support groups with the members being accountable to one another.

They confessed their faults to one another (See James 5:16) *prayed for each another and stirred up one another to love and good works*.

In 1738 (interestingly on December 25th) Rules for the Band Societies were drawn up. It consisted of 11 questions that could be asked of each other as often as occasion offers. However: the following four questions were asked of everyone at every weekly meeting.

What known sins have you committed since our last meeting? What temptations have you met with? How were you delivered? What have you thought, said, or done, of which you doubt whether it be sin or not?

What will we be thinking about this coming Christmas Day?

Accountability, speaks of 'being answerable' to someone – being transparent. As Christians we conduct our lives knowing we are accountable to God and others. Everyone will be accountable to God on Judgement Day, whether they realise this or not.

Accountability is about *accepting responsibility for our own actions and behaviour* – admitting when we are wrong, and shows an ownership and willingness to admit when we have made mistakes.

Proverbs 27:17 explains – "As iron sharpens iron, so one man sharpens another." Accountability can put us in a vulnerable position, but it is this process of discipleship that makes us strong and mature. Sharing life with one another in Church goes deeper than just worshipping and witnessing together.

Proverbs 12:15 – "The way of a fool seems right to him, but a wise man listens to advice." God has given us one another so we can share counsel, listen to, guide, and come alongside each other. Don't struggle on your own in tough decisions and dilemmas in your life.

I have made it a practice to build in 'accountability people' into my life – especially in positions of leadership. During my years as a Pastor, I asked another Deacon (various, as the leadership changed) to be my accountability person.

With specific reference to Church and Leaders meetings – I invited and gave them permission to tell me if they thought I came over in the wrong spirit – spoke out of turn ... or whatever!

I did the same when I was leading a worship band. Others were not aware I had an accountability person. It is up to us individually to build these principles into our lives. We need to practice accountability as Christians – whether we are leaders or not.

I recommend the principle of finding a prayer partner where you can meet regularly, share openly, pray specifically – and take people and situations to the foot of the Cross of Christ. This is the place where we can bring our burdens to Jesus. We lay them down at the Cross of Christ – leave them and the outcome with Him – walk away – and stand strong again in His grace, peace, and forgiveness. David the psalmist wrote, "Cast your care on the LORD and He will sustain you; He will never let the righteous fall." (Psalm 55:22)

Our inner struggles and problems can be shared in confidence with each other – but everything is before God. Jesus alone is the One who enables us to live in freedom and victory. At times, just sharing, speaking out and verbalising my concerns and feelings with my prayer partner, the Holy Spirit brings me to that place of perspective. (I.e. – the thought I had about a person or situation was not justified – confirms motives, attitudes, and desires – or confirms direction and decisions to take.)

Integrity in Reliability.

God is ever true and always faithful to His promises to us. We are to keep our word also, of those things that we promise or offer to others. "It is better to say nothing than to make a promise and not keep it." (Ecclesiastes 5:5 – New Living Translation)

Integrity in Confidentiality.

The wisdom given in the book of Proverbs has much to say concerning how we should handle personal information that we know or discover about other people.

Proverbs 11:13 – "A gossip betrays a confidence, but a trustworthy man keeps a secret." There may be times when someone says to us, "I need to share this but don't tell anyone..." *We must not put ourselves in this position without clarification. We need to say that we may need to share with someone ... or suggest what they may need to do ... if it affects their (or others) care, well-being, and safety.*

Proverbs 25:9-10 (The Message Bible) – "In the heat of an argument, don't betray confidences; word is sure to get around, and no one will trust you."

Proverbs 17:9 (The Amplified Bible) – "He who covers and

forgives an offense seeks love, but he who repeats or harps on a matter separates even close friends."

When people know they have been talked about, when personal information about them has been revealed which was confidential – feelings are hurt, trust is destroyed and relationships ruined.

For me personally, any information I learn about a person when I am meeting them one to one – I will treat as confidential – unless we have agreed on what aspects are okay to share.

There will be times, when other people need to be aware of certain circumstances in the lives of those who may require ongoing pastoral care. *Share only on a need-to-know basis. Consider which person or people can help the best in each situation.*

Ask yourself, "Am I committed to being part of the solution?" How can I help or serve this person? Am I willing and able to offer the support and care required?" Also reflect on – "Why do I need to talk to others about this person's situation?" If in doubt, check and ask – "Is this news, information and update confidential?"

"Whoever walks in integrity walks securely…" (Proverbs 10:9) May the Lord Jesus continue to help us as His disciples to walk the route of integrity as we seek to bring glory to Him in these aspects of our lives.

Reflection for prayer and action.

- Do I build accountability procedures into my life and relationships?
- Use the Lord's prayer and consider the specific words, 'And lead us not into temptation, but deliver us from the evil one.' We all have areas of weakness and vulnerability that we need to watch out for. If there is a specific sin that we find ourselves asking forgiveness for, time and time again (a destructive habit or wrong way of speaking or thinking) – get some help and counsel. Confide with a close fellow believer and ask for prayer. The Holy Spirit who dwells within us as Christians – is both powerful and Holy, and He enables us to live our lives pleasing and glorifying to Jesus.
- Is there any action I need to take, to keep my word of promise I have made to someone?
- Consider your principles and practices re confidentiality. Ask for God's wisdom to guide and help you, as you support, care, and encourage those in need.

8 The Track of Testing

Readings – James 1:1-18 / Luke 4:1-12

Most of us will acknowledge that living as a disciple of Jesus – our times of testing can prove very difficult. The Refiner's fire, or the place of suffering for Christ's sake, is challenging, and yet it is where we grow the most and learn things of true worth and value, for ourselves and to share with others.

Testing will come in numerous ways, many of which we have no control over – like health issues, family matters and work-related issues. All of these will also affect our spiritual lives.

God wants to use these occasions for us to draw closer to Him, to put our full trust in Him and to improve and nurture us in our faith.

God desires to test our faith – so our trust and confidence in His goodness, faithfulness and promises – is genuine. He could answer all our prayers at a click of His finger, but our faith will grow stronger through the tough times and seasons of waiting – as we learn to fully rely on the Lord.

James says (1:2-4) we are to "...consider it pure joy, whenever you face trials of many kinds, because you know that the testing of your faith develops perseverance. Perseverance must finish its work so that you may be mature and complete, not lacking anything."

The joy is not in the trial, but in the end result – that trials develop perseverance making us mature and complete.

Hebrews 12:2-3 explains, “Jesus for the joy set before Him endured the cross, scorning its shame and sat down at the right hand of the throne of God. Consider Him who endured such opposition from sinful men, so that you will not grow weary and lose heart.”

Jeremiah the prophet heard from God concerning times of testing and declared these words.

Jeremiah 9:7 – Therefore this is what the LORD Almighty says: “See, I will refine and test them, for what else can I do because of the sin of my people.”

Jeremiah 11:20 – “But O Lord Almighty, You who judge righteously, and test the heart and mind...”

Jeremiah 12:3 – “Yet You know me O Lord, You see me and test my thoughts about You.”

In Luke 4:1-4 – we read that Jesus was full of the Holy Spirit when He was led by the Spirit into the desert where He would be tempted by the devil for forty days.

The place of abundant life, fruitfulness, and effectiveness for the Christian, is only possible when we are full of the Holy Spirit of God, and being led by Him.

Being full of the Holy Spirit, Jesus overcame the devil's temptations – which came as cunning lies as Satan misquoted God's Word. Testing may come to us in our place of weakness (sin) or place of strength. (pride and ego) An acronym for Ego is ‘Edging God Out.’ Daily, we need to ensure that we trust Jesus in all things, and keep Him at the centre of all our conversations and activities.

Testing often comes in the place of Change!

It may arise when we are feeling down. We would do well to pause … to reflect and pray – on those occasions when we are feeling anxious, angry, lonely, or tired. It is easy to make a wrong decision, or speak and act in a wrong spirit when we are too busy – or going through a difficult time ourselves.

Testing may also turn up in our times of rejoicing and victory – just when everything is going well and you are walking a smooth road. Testing can also come our way when we choose to make any move to be pleasing to God and draw nearer to Him. Our enemy Satan, is prowling around like a roaring lion, seeking to trip us and trap us into temptation.

The place of testing is the time when we are to be open to God's Word.

We need to know God's Word well! We cannot live by bread alone, but by every word that proceeds from the mouth of God. (See Matthew 4:4)

The devil knows the scriptures. We need to devote ourselves to the study of them, so we know them better. (in context, word meanings as they were written etc...)

If God's Word is our priority, then we must continually trust what He says in His Word – when it's all we've got left, at those times when everything else seems to have been stripped away from us.

James 1:12 – "Blessed (happy to be envied) is the man who perseveres under trial, because when he has stood the test, he will receive the crown of life that God has promised to those who love Him."

The Crown of life is our Salvation and hope of Eternal life. We take up the cross daily to follow, love and serve Jesus in this life – but we will wear the Crown of Life forever.

The next part of Jesus' temptation is recorded in Luke 4:5-8. The devil said to Jesus "Worship me, and the World's Kingdoms will be yours." (They already belonged to Jesus)

This type of testing speaks about us doing God's work in our way and not His way. The worship of power, success and status is not compatible with the worship of God.

There is a warning for the Church here also, that we must seek God, discern and carry out His plans and purposes and not just ask His blessing on our good ideas, agendas and programmes.

Is our praying more about my/our success, or about God's honour and purposes? The path to the Kingdom of God involves humble sacrifice, not worldly power or recognition. James reminds us (1:13-14) that when tempted, no one should say "God is tempting me." For God cannot be tempted by evil, nor does He tempt anyone; but each one is tempted when by his own evil desire, he is dragged away and enticed.

Watch out for the enemy's subtle deception. Sometimes our desires may not be evil; just selfish (what I want rather than what God wants) but they can still drag us away from God's best and highest call for our lives.

The final temptation for Jesus in Luke 4:9-13 is when the devil quoted the scripture saying "If you are the Son of God, stand on the highest point of the temple, throw yourself down and God will protect you." Jesus replied, "Do not put the Lord your God to the test." This command was given in Deuteronomy 6:16-18- "Do not test the Lord your God ... be sure to keep the commands of the Lord your God ... do what is right and good in the Lord's sight..." Jesus continues to show how the Word of God can be used as a weapon to overcome the strategies of Satan. Paul also reminds us in Ephesians 6:17 that the Word of God is the Sword of the Spirit – part of the armour of God that we must put on daily.

God will only permit what He can use for His glory, when we are surrendered to Him. We know that in all things God works for the good of those who love Him, who have been called according to His purpose. (See Romans 8:28)

In 1 Corinthians 10:13 we are promised that, "No temptation has seized you, except what is common to man. And God is faithful; *He will not let you be tempted beyond what you can bear.* But when you are tempted, He will also provide a way out so that you can stand up under it."

In 2 Corinthians 13:5-6 – Paul wrote, "Examine yourselves to see whether you are in the faith, test yourselves ..." He goes on to say that if we realise that Christ Jesus is in us, ... he trusts that we will discover that we have not failed the test.

Reflection for prayer and action.

- Times of testing and trial are times when God is working on our maturity. Paul declared in Romans 8:28 – "And we know that in all things God works for the good of those who love Him, who have been called according to His purpose." If you are finding it hard to understand or see the goodness of God in your circumstances, turn this into a prayer. 'Lord, please reveal your good and greater purpose in what I am going through. Help me to keep trusting You.' God has promised that He is watching over His word to accomplish it. (See Jeremiah 1:12)
- Think on those times when you have been tested. What lessons did you learn? – that you could share with others who are going through difficult trials.
- Put on the armour of God each day. The belt of truth – the breastplate of righteousness – feet fitted with readiness from the gospel of peace. Take up the shield of faith, the helmet of salvation, the sword of the Spirit (God's Word) and pray in the Spirit on all occasions with all kinds of prayers and requests. (Read Ephesians 6:10-18)

The Street of Selflessness

Reading – Philippians 2:1-11

As we continue to journey as followers of Jesus Christ, we learn how to live life God's way and then model and example that through our worship to God and in our relationships with one another.

Let us consider another vital step in discipleship as we walk along the 'Street of Selflessness.'

What does selflessness mean to you?

Dictionary definitions include being oblivious to self, incapable of selfishness, generous, self-denying, self-sacrificing, unselfish concern for the welfare of others.

The Street of Selflessness is part of the most excellent way to live.

In 1 Corinthians 13 – Paul writes (in the context of spiritual gifts and being part of the body of Christ) – "I will show you the most excellent way."

As part of that most excellent way he says that Love, {which is the greatest} *is not self-seeking.* (1 Cor 13:5)

On every occasion when we may be tempted to live for self, God's Word reveals the way of our higher calling. Psalm 119:36-37 says "Turn my heart towards your statutes and not towards selfish gain. Turn my eyes away from worthless things; renew my life according to your word." (or Life in Your Way)

The words of Frank Sinatra's famous song 'My Way' declare, "I did what I had to do and saw it through without exemption. I planned each charted course, each careful step along the by-way, and more, much more than this, I did it my way."

Paul Anka who first heard the original French song in 1967, re-wrote it quoting that he wrote it as it was because we were in the 'me generation' – 'me this' and 'me that.' Nothing has changed!

As disciples of Jesus – we seek to do everything 'God's Way.' God's ways and plans for our lives will always be the best. David the psalmist declared, "As for God, His way is perfect; the word of the LORD is flawless. (Psalm 18:30)

The Street of Selflessness leads us away from selfish ambition.

In Galatians 5, before Paul reminds us of the Fruit of the Holy Spirit (v 22-23) he lists the acts of the sinful nature which are contrary to the Spirit – one of them being 'selfish ambition.'

Ambition for Christians is good and right – when it is God focussed and for His glory. I have always been encouraged by the ambition verse in 1 Thessalonians 4:11-12 – "Make it your ambition to lead a quiet life, to mind your own business and to work with your hands just as we told you, so that your daily life may win the respect of outsiders and so that you will not be dependent on anybody."

Paul was sharing this in the context of living to please God. This is what selflessness is all about. Living for Jesus Christ is; emptying ourselves of self, as we seek first God's Kingdom (His rule, reign, and purposes) and His righteousness.

James warns us (3: v16) "...For where you have selfish ambition, there you will find disorder and every evil practice."

1 Corinthians 3:6-7 – The apostle Paul is rebuking divisions in the Church and says – "I planted the seed, Apollos watered it, but God made it grow. So, neither he who plants nor he who waters is anything, but only God, who make things grow." It is God alone who makes our lives and ministries fruitful and effective, and all the glory must be ascribed to Him.

Selflessness will always give the Glory to God.

Let us remind ourselves again to watch those areas of self, where we can become over confident because of our gifting and ability – those things we can do without thinking, planning, practice, or trying too hard.

Hand them back to the Lord and ask Him to bless, quicken and sharpen those skills you already have. {Acknowledge His gifts to you and give God the glory and praise}

Walking the Street of Selflessness will enable us to consider others better than ourselves.

Philippians 2:3-4 says "Do nothing out of selfish ambition or vain conceit (our notion of ourselves) but in humility consider others better than yourselves."

We need to have a right opinion of ourselves of who we are in Christ. We are worthy – accepted – dearly loved. Being humble and selfless is not having a low opinion of yourself. Seeing ourselves as Christ sees us – enables us to consider others better than ourselves.

v 4 says that "Each of you should not only look to your own interests *but also* to the interests of others.

To work, minister, pray and communicate effectively we all need to look after our own interests in addition to looking to the interests of others. We need to ensure we take time out for ourselves; building ourselves up, resting and relaxing, learning to say 'No' at times – so that we do not burn out – or our yoke will become too heavy.

Making time for your marriage, your family, your quiet times with God ... is a must, if you are to serve others well.

Walking the Street of Selflessness requires that we take on the same attitude as Jesus.

Philippians 2:5 – "Your attitude should be the same as that of Christ Jesus." Although being in very nature God (God Himself) Jesus did not grasp His rights and authority but He made himself a servant for us.

He made himself nothing, and humbled himself in obedience. Obedience to His Father took Jesus to the cross.

The evidence of selflessness is looking for ways in which we can serve one another and then doing it.

Jesus told His disciples in Mark 9:35 – "If anyone wants to be first, he must be the very last, and the servant of all." Jesus said again in Matthew 23:11-12, "The greatest among you will be your servant. For whoever exalts himself will be humbled, and whoever humbles himself will be exalted."

What Jesus said, is what Jesus would do.

Every day we face the choice to do things God's way or our way. We need to daily die to ourselves, surrender our will and choices to the Lord and as we do, the life of Jesus is evident within us.

One of the main points of my life-story is that 'Jesus saved me – from myself.' I often reflect as to what I might be doing and experiencing today, if God had not stepped in to rescue me from my selfishness and the brokenness that brings. Our lives can be easily shattered and bring disappointment when we choose to do things our way. Christian conversion is all about self decreasing and Christ increasing.

On the Street of Selflessness, we fix our eyes on Jesus and follow Him.

Jesus said to His disciples (Matt 16:24-25) "If anyone would come after me, he must deny himself and take up his cross and follow me. For whoever wants to save his life will lose it, but whoever loses his life for me will find it."

Jesus went on to say in Matthew 19:29 – "And everyone who has left houses or brothers or sisters or father or mother or children or fields for my sake will receive a hundred times as much and will inherit eternal life."

God, through His Word – often gives encouragement to us in following the ways of discipleship. (pointing out our eternal reward, our crown, and our prize in the Kingdom of Heaven)

Our joy should be in serving God for who He is, not for what He does. If we do not spend time in cultivating our love relationship with Jesus Christ, we will not be able to serve others effectively. Everything flows out of God's love for us and in us. As we love, worship, and obey Jesus – our love and service to others will follow.

2 Timothy 3:2-3 – lists eighteen things that result when self reigns. "In the last days people will be lovers of themselves, lovers of money, boastful, proud, abusive, disobedient to parents, ungrateful, unholy, without love, unforgiving, slanderous, without self-control, brutal, not lovers of good, treacherous, rash, conceited, lovers of pleasure rather than lovers of God.

Colossians 3:1-2 reminds us to "....Set your hearts on things above, where Christ is seated at the right hand of God. Set your minds on things above, not on earthly things. For you died and your life is now hidden with Christ in God." Our old nature (wanting to please only ourselves) has died – and our new nature and identity is now in Jesus Christ – in God, and we are secure and confident in our salvation.

One of the characteristics that God gives to us through the Fruit of His Holy Spirit is self-control. Enabled by the power of God's Spirit, we can bring our selfish actions, reactions, and desires under God's control.

May the Lord enable each of us to live for Him and others.

Reflection for prayer and action.

- Ask the Lord to bring an opportunity to you this week where you can serve others.
- In your prayers of petition and intercession, ask that God will be honoured and glorified in the way He answers them.
- Ask the Holy Spirit for His strength and power to enable you to stay close to Jesus and to do what He asks of you.
- Opportunities or requests to help, support and encourage people in need can often arise when we are busy, tired, or at a time which is inconvenient. Ask God for His strength, grace, and wisdom, to guide you as you seek to serve Him and others.
- Do you need to take some time-out to address some interests in your own life? When we are active in serving others, it can be easy to neglect our own work and family responsibilities and miss out on our devotional time with Jesus – because we are too busy. To serve others effectively we need to ensure we take regular time to rest, relax, reflect, and pray.

10 The Way of Words

Reading – James 3:1-12

We continue our discipleship walk looking at the importance of our words and speech. I was thinking of some things we say concerning our words in conversation. "I don't know what to say. I'm speechless! How can I say this?"

Do you recall the song by F.R David called, 'Words don't come easy – to me'? There are many occasions when we just cannot find words to share, and yet our tongue (that can produce 90 words per minute!) is probably what causes us to sin and stumble the most in the way we speak to, or about others.

James 3 – is the main chapter that deals with 'taming the tongue', but the tongue is mentioned in each of the five chapters of the book. James describes the tongue as boastful, a fire, a world of restless evil, corruptive and poisonous.

I recall seeing a photograph of thousands of scattered feathers in a field. Our words are like feathers blown in the wind. They are very hard to retract once released.

With our words we can communicate love, joy, encouragement – share the Good News – but with our words we can also criticise, tear down and discourage.

In context, James is sharing that not many should presume to be teachers – as they will be judged more strictly. I do not claim to be a Bible teacher, but as a preacher of the gospel of Jesus, I still sense a huge responsibility with the choice of words that I share in preaching, and to ensure that God's truth is proclaimed through and in my words.

In 1 Timothy 3:1-13 and Titus 1:5-9 we can read about the specific characteristics required for those who serve in Church leadership as elders and deacons. When it comes to what we say and how we communicate – it is vital for a Church leader to be 'watchful of their words' – but this also applies to each of us as disciples of Jesus.

1 Timothy 4:12b says "*...set an example for the believers in speech*, in life, in love, in faith and in purity."

Titus 2:7b-8a "...In your teaching show integrity, seriousness and *soundness of speech that cannot be condemned...*"

James says that if anyone is never at fault in what they say, they are perfect – able to keep their whole body in check (v2) He gives vivid descriptions of things in life that show the power of the tongue. A small bit in a horse's mouth makes them obey and can turn the whole animal. Our tongue is like a bit. If we could restrain our tongue, we could control our whole body.

A huge ship, driven by the winds is steered by a small rudder. Like the pilot, you choose the course you will go with your words. Will they build up and give courage, or condemn and destroy? The tongue may be small in size – but its words can have huge impact for better or worse. We must be watchful that our words do not manipulate, dominate, or control others.

The tongue is small, but makes great boasts and exercises great power. The only boasting a Christian should do – is like the song says, "I will boast in Jesus Christ, His death and resurrection."

Everything we have and do, is because of God's grace and provision. Every answered prayer is for the glory of God. Every gift, talent, and ability we possess – is God given.

We need to watch what we allow into our hearts. This commences with what we think about – for our thoughts can soon be expressed in our words. If we were to keep thinking we are unworthy, rather than accept the love and forgiveness that God offers, our words will start to express those feelings.

Jesus said in Matthew 12:34b – *"For out of the overflow of the heart the mouth speaks."*

What are we storing up in our hearts? If we store up unforgiveness in our heart, then unforgiveness and bitterness will come out in our words and actions. If we store up encouragement – encouragement will overflow.

Later in Matthew 15:18 – Jesus says again the same truth but in reverse. "But the things that come out of the mouth come from the heart, and these make a man unclean."

Ephesians 4:29 – "Do not let any unwholesome talk come out of your mouths, but only what is helpful for building others up according to their needs, that it may benefit those who listen."

James goes on to give a further illustration, to warn us

concerning the destruction that wrong words can bring. 'A small spark to a flame will destroy a great forest.' Just like striking a match – negative and critical words spoken – soon ignite to become a raging fire of destruction.

Words are the most powerful thing
we can use for good or evil.

Jesus reminds us "But I tell you that men will have to give account on the day of judgement for every careless word they have spoken. For by your words you will be acquitted, and by your words you will be condemned." (Matt 12:36-37)

James reminds us (3:8) – "that no man can tame the tongue." But the Holy Spirit enables us to watch our words and grant us self-control rather than act and react with wrong words and actions.

v9 – "With the tongue we praise our Lord and Father, and with it we curse men who have been made in God's likeness. Out of the same mouth come praise and cursing. My brothers – this should not be!"

James uses illustrations from nature to show that being double tongued should not be, but also in fact – is impossible. He asks, "Can both fresh water and salt water flow from the same spring?"

An untamed tongue at its worst, will wrecks lives, break hearts, and ruin reputations.

What can we do to tame the tongue?

Let us look at some further scriptures and some practical applications that will help us.

James says in chapter 1:19 – "My dear brothers, take note of this: "Everyone should *be quick to listen, slow to speak and slow to become angry*,..." Later (5:9) – James adds – "*Don't grumble against each other*, brothers or you will be judged. The Judge is standing at the door."

Negative, critical, and judging words are usually a trespass against another person, but in so doing – we also sin against God. We need to be open to God's discipline and correction. As with any sin, if we admit and confess our sin – God is faithful and just and He will forgive us.

It is in this aspect of our words, that whenever possible, we need to also ask forgiveness of the person we have spoken against.

Another point we need to consider is – the manner and tone in which we speak. I recall the song "It ain't *what* you do it's *the way* that you do it." So, with our words sometimes, "It's not *what* you say, but *the way* that you say it."

When we look at the fruit of the Holy Spirit in Galatians 5:22-23 – we discover our words need to be loving – impart joy and peace, express kindness and goodness, be faithful words – that are also full of faith – spoken with gentleness, and finally we need self-control over what we say to enable us to keep quiet at certain times.

(Ecclesiastes 3:7b reminds us – *there is a time to be silent and a time to speak*)

There will of course be occasions where we do have to correct, instruct, advise, and give feedback about people and situations. When we do; keep all these things in mind, and don't just do it in love – but do it 'because you love' – and in humility.

James 1:26 – "If anyone considers himself religious and yet does not keep a tight rein on his tongue, he deceives himself and his religion is worthless."

Watching our words is a practice
- it will not just happen.

If we seek the Holy Spirit on this matter, He will reveal if our words need to be fewer – and/or more selective.

We need to 'practice more' the right use of our tongues that James mentions in 3:9 … to praise our LORD and Father, but also to express appreciation and encouragement to others.

"*Let your conversation be always full of grace, seasoned with salt*, so that you may know how to answer everyone." (Colossians 4:6)

Reflection for prayer and action.

- What attitudes and feelings have I expressed through my words over this last week?
- When we are tempted to grumble or criticise either a person or situation – cultivate the practice of turning it into a prayer. Commend them to God's grace and ask Him to bless their lives.
- Ask the Lord to help you speak words that will edify and be a blessing to others, that will witness to our changed lives as disciples of Jesus.
- Look afresh at the nine characteristics of the Fruit of the Holy Spirit listed in Galatians 5:22-23. *Are these fruit of the Spirit qualities evident in my daily conversations?* "The right word at the right time is like a custom-made piece of jewelry." – Proverbs 25:11 – The Message Bible.

The Trail of Transformation

Reading – Romans 12:1-21

What words come to your mind when you hear the word transformation?

Dictionary definitions will include change, alteration, conversion, remodel, revolutionise – to make or become different.

The Christian life is a transition to continued transformation.

Romans 12:2 instructs us, "Do not conform any longer to the pattern of this world, but be transformed by the renewing of your mind." We are transformed and changed to being more like Jesus as we think and act upon God's word. As disciples, we will be walking daily along the trail of transformation – as this is a lifelong process.

Most of us dislike change. Some of us fear it, avoid it, and even run from it – yet as Christians, we must learn to welcome and embrace it, as the road of discipleship involves continual change.

Jesus said to His disciples "I tell you the truth, unless you change, and become like little children, you will never enter the kingdom of heaven." {Matthew 18:3}

We need to change and to become child-like – approaching God humbly and trusting fully in our heavenly Father's provision, care and love for us.

Walking the trail of transformation means we choose to change the way we think.

It is only as we change our thinking that we will change our actions, behaviour, and habits. Before we were Christians, life was all about us, but now our thinking must be focussed on Jesus. What would He do, think and say?

2 Corinthians 5:17 – "Therefore, if anyone is in Christ, he is a new creation; the old has gone, the new has come!"

Picture a house in your mind which requires repair and attention. We may try to paint over or put filler into rotten wood – when what is needed is a completely new replacement. God does not patch up our old life – He transforms it into 'New life in Christ.'

When we become Christians and accept Jesus as our Lord and Saviour, we become a new creation. This means we are not the same as we were; we are not a remake of the old person! We may still look the same on the outside, and we do have to renew our mind daily (change our thinking) but inside spiritually, we are new!

Transformation is a total change in heart attitude.

1 Samuel 16:7 reminds us that the LORD does not look at the things man looks at. Man looks at the outward appearance, but the LORD looks at the heart.

The trail of transformation leads us away from conforming to the patterns of this world to conforming to the image of Jesus Christ.

The goal in Christian living is to be conformed to the likeness of Jesus. Romans 8:29 in The Message Bible reads, "God knew what He was doing from the very beginning. He decided from the outset to shape the lives of those who love Him along the same lines as the life of His Son."

The Greek word of transformed – means to change into another form. The word metamorphosis is derived from this word, which we use to describe the process of a caterpillar changing into a butterfly.

> Walking the trail of transformation will enable us to test and approve what God's good, pleasing, and perfect will is.

Discerning God's will is one of the vital characteristics of Christian discipleship. When we discover it; and obey what God is telling us to do, we will find our highest purpose, meaning and fulfilment in life.

Romans 12:2 tells us that as our thinking is transformed, we will know God's good, pleasing, and perfect will. *Disobedience can cloud our thinking.*

Years of clogging up our minds with negative and destructive images and attitudes, will not be helpful when we want to discern God's perfect will. (either for ourselves or if we are interceding in prayer for others)

God reveals His will to us as written in the Bible, through the Holy Spirit speaking to our heart and conscience, and He also speaks to us as we listen to the counsel of other Christians.

In addition, we must be actively seeking God's will and what He wants to teach us in each circumstance that comes our way.

The transformation of your mind (thinking) means putting on your new self.

We must actively choose to put on the new self. Ephesians 4:24 "...put off your old self, which is being corrupted by its deceitful desires; to be made new in the attitude of your minds; and to *put on the new self, created to be like God in true righteousness and holiness*."

Verses 25-30 tell us the areas where we need to re-think about where we are at – and ask for the Holy Spirit's transforming power to help us.

We are to put off falsehood. Speak truthfully to your neighbour. Don't sin by getting angry – don't give the devil a foothold. Steal no longer. Work – do something useful with your hands so you have something to share with those in need.

Do not let unwholesome talk come out of your mouth – but only what is helpful for building others up according to their needs. Do not grieve the Holy Spirit. Get rid of bitterness, rage, anger, brawling and slander, along with every form of malice – be kind and compassionate to one another, forgiving each other just as in Christ, God has forgiven you.

God is the One who transforms our attitudes. He alone can change the heart of any human being. In Ezra 6:22 we read that, "The Lord had filled (the Israelites) with joy by *changing the attitude of the king of Assyria*, so that he assisted them in the work on the house of God ..."

Colossians 3:9 reminds us – you have taken off your old self with its practices and have put on the new self, which is being renewed in knowledge in the image of its Creator. We are being transformed into renewed people – to the glory of God.

The trail of transformation will cause us to behold and gaze upon the glory of the LORD.

2 Corinthians 3:18 – "we ... all reflect the Lord's glory, and are being transformed (this is progressive) into His likeness with ever increasing glory, which comes from the Lord, who is the Spirit."

Being in – and feeling God's presence – is the place where transformation takes place.

As we seek Jesus and fix our eyes on Him – keep Him at the centre of all we do – He will transform us. As we read and think on scripture, seek God in prayer and quiet reflection – He will transform us.

The glory of the LORD that caused the face of Moses to shine, is the glory that transforms us.

John 1:14 – "The Word became flesh and lived for a while among us. We have seen His glory, the glory of the one and only Son, who came from the Father, full of grace and truth."

May our lives witness to others that we have been truly changed and transformed by Jesus. Rather than blending in with the ways of the world, may our lives shine the light of Christ into the darkness of this world.

Reflection for prayer and action.

- Ask for God's help to enable you encounter change in a positive way.
- Take time to seek the Lord's perfect will for your life at this time. Ask the question – "Am I using my time and gifts in the most fruitful way?
- Seek to live in the Lord's presence each hour of the day. Acknowledge Him in every situation.
- On our journey of discipleship – we are all a continued work in progress. (*We are like a piece of clay, and Jesus is the Potter – who lovingly shapes and transforms us, so we display His glory.*) Reflect on the last year and ask: "Have I continued to grow in my relationship with Jesus and my love for Him? In what ways has the Word of God transformed my thinking, speaking and actions?"

12

The Freeway of Faith and Works

Be Doers of the Word in Faith!

Reading – James 1:19-25 / 2:14-26

As we keep on keeping on in our walk of discipleship, let us consider the importance of why faith and works (deeds) must grow together in our lives, and then look at ways in which we can become doers of the Word, and not just hearers.

I have a happy announcement to share with you. "Faith and works are happily married together. Please don't try to separate them!"

This chapter of writing, (like every message we hear) will only become more information and knowledge, if we do not choose to do something with what we've heard.

In the parable of the talents, Jesus challenges us on the question "What will you do with what you've got?" (our gifts, time, money...)

In this passage of scripture in James, the LORD is challenging us with the question, "What will you do, with what you've heard?" We are told to be slow to speak and slow to become angry but quick to listen. Listening to God's Word, listening for God's voice is vital, but the changing point comes when we act on what God says – in faith and obedience.

In James' imaginary conversation between two people, he says in 2:17 "...faith by itself if it is not accompanied by action is dead." And later in 2:8b – "I will show you my faith by what I do."

I have written and delivered a good number of sermons on faith; and a few on social works and action – but I'm understanding more, concerning the need to walk the Freeway of Faith and works together.

We can see an illustration of faith and works functioning together, every time we go for a walk. We put our left foot forward (faith) then the right foot (works) If we did not follow faith with works – we would be hopping!

> We must have an experience with
> God, from what we believe.

The Bible reminds us of the importance of renewing our minds. (You may have noticed how this theme of 'renewing and changing our thinking' has been key – in several of the chapters of this book)

If we desire to see changes in our lives it will commence when we start to think differently, and as a result we will live differently. We need to align our thinking in accordance with God's Word. Renewal comes as our faith in what God says and promises becomes our experience.

When God reveals something from His Word that catches our attention or speaks to our minds – He wants that truth or command to work into our experience and acts of obedience. Faith and works together – is a Faith that works.

Every sermon and bible study should lead us to prayer,

where we ask God to help us act in some way on what He is telling us. Or if it is a principle that we already do – we can ask ourselves, "How can I improve or become more effective and fruitful?"

Therefore, I believe in a time for prayer and reflection following a sermon – where we can make that initial choice to do something in response to the message – while it is fresh in our minds.

What action could we take this week to apply God's Word to our daily lives? May the Holy Spirit make us aware of opportunities where we can bless our neighbours and communities, as we live out the Good News of the Gospel – in our words and works.

Paul, as well as James, reminds us of the importance of faith and works together. Ephesians 2:10 says, "For we are God's workmanship, created in Christ Jesus to do good works, which God prepared in advance for us to do."

It is important to remember that 'we are not saved by our good works, nor do we gain any more favour with God through doing good works.'

Love God first with all your heart and
He will give you His works to do.

James reminds us (1:23-24) "...don't be like the man who looks at his face in the mirror and after going away, immediately forgets what he looks like." Do what God says in His Word. At the wedding in Cana of Galilee, prior to the miracle of Jesus changing water into the best wine, His mother Mary had informed the servants, “Do whatever He tells you.” (See John 2:5)

In our practical works, but also in our spiritual ministries, God wants us to experience the reality of His power within us as we trust in Him.

Our faith grows and strengthens as God takes us into new, challenging, and fruitful areas of ministry and serving. We are blessed and encouraged as we seek to become participators and more involved within worship and ministry – rather than being just spectators.

You may feel that you are not equipped or qualified to do a task – thinking, ‘There is someone else who can do it better than me!’ God equips us to do, what He calls us to do.

Jesus understands that sharing our faith in Him with others and witnessing to the truth of God’s word is costly, challenging, and difficult. That is why He sent His promised Holy Spirit.

Jesus said, “But you will receive power when the Holy Spirit comes on you; and you will be my witnesses .... “(Acts 1:8)

Most Churches will agree that witnessing and evangelism must be their main purpose for ministry, therefore we need to pray intentionally for opportunities to share our story of faith in God, serve others, and account for the hope of Jesus who lives in us.

As those occasions arise – trust the Spirit of God to empower you with wise words, the right spirit and a loving and compassionate heart.

Spiritual gifts also need to be passionately pursued. Paul reminds us – "Eagerly desire spiritual gifts – especially prophecy" (See 1 Corinthians 14:1)

If any of you lack wisdom, he should ask God who gives generously to all without finding fault; and it will be given him. (James 1:5) We tend to think that if God wants us to have a spiritual gift, He will just put it our way. Be encouraged to ask away – for God's wisdom and gifts!

Jesus said, "If you, then, though you are evil, know how to give good gifts to your children, how much more will your Father in heaven give good gifts to those who ask Him." (Matthew 7:11)

In all our praying and petitions, we are to ask that the Name of Jesus will be honoured and glorified.

Reflection for prayer and action.

- In prayer, ask Jesus for a fresh touch from the Holy Spirit upon your life. Is there anything in our lives that is holding us back from being fully committed to following Jesus? Surrender your life afresh to being a disciple and follower of Jesus. The Holy Spirit is both holy and powerful. He also guides and goads us into the ways of truth and obedience to God's Word. He will enable you to become more like Jesus and empower you in the works that God calls you to do. The Holy Spirit reveals the truth and ways of Christ to us. Jesus said, "The Spirit will take from what is mine and make it known to you." (John 16:15b)
- What will you do in response to this message you have read?
- Is there a spiritual gift you need to ask God for, to enable you to be more effective and fruitful in your life and ministry? Come and ask from your loving and generous Heavenly Father.
- Ask Jesus to help you live for Him by your faith and works.

Words for the Journey

In this short book of sermons, we have considered some key topics of discipleship. Like any message, they cannot cover every aspect of the theme within the time allotted. I often say – '…that will be the subject for another sermon!' I hope this book will make you think further on these characteristics of what it is to be a disciple of Jesus.

As you journey on to the end of your life (or until Jesus comes again) the Holy Spirit, our Teacher, Counsellor, and Guide – will reveal further aspects of discipleship to each of us.

In conclusion, I would like to share with you some specific discipleship lessons that I was reminded of during the Covid 19 pandemic and the times of national and global lockdowns in 2020-2021.

From early 2022, all covid restrictions were lifted in England, and we are now in the days that have been referred to as 'learning to live with covid.'

As Church life and activities have now resumed, I try to remind myself regularly of the things I noted during the time when normal day to day life ceased; when churches were unable to open, and all the daily things we took for granted were only future possibilities.

Whatever happens to us personally, nationally, or globally as Christians – God always wants to speak to us. He never leaves us or forsakes us. Our mission – to make Jesus known and live for Him – remains the same through all the changing scenes of life.

Throughout those early days of lock-down, Covid was the dominating news, day after day. We were all living through unprecedented times, uncharted waters, and this was also a great challenge to the world Governments and Medical professions.

Covid 19 was a CORONA virus. As Covid updates continued to hit the daily headlines, I felt led to work out an 'acronym' for the word Corona, which would help me refocus on the Lord within this global event. I came up with:

"Christ Only – Rules Over Nations – Always!"

It is good to remember that God is Sovereign, LORD and King of heaven and earth – but also, over every single detail and circumstance of your life. The LORD Reigns!

As we read or memorise scripture, the Holy Spirit will quicken its meaning to us, or bring it to our remembrance when we need comfort, hope or direction. Two verses spoke to me specifically in those early days of lock-down.

In Mathew 6:34 Jesus said, "Therefore, do not worry about tomorrow, for tomorrow will worry about itself. Each day has enough trouble of its own."

The fears of tomorrow, can rob us of the peace that Jesus gives for 'this day.' Jesus taught His disciples, "Give us each day our daily bread." (Luke 11:3)

The other verses are found in James 4:13-16. "Come now, you who say – Today or tomorrow we will go into such and such a town and spend a year there and trade and make a profit – yet you do not know what tomorrow will bring. What is your life? For you are a mist that appears for a little time and then vanishes. Instead, you ought to say – '*If the Lord wills*, we will live and do this or that.' As it is, you boast in your arrogance. All such boasting is evil."

Each moment, each hour and day is a gift from God. As disciples of Jesus, we need to continue to acknowledge that everything we do – is always *God willing*. We are not to assume anything or take things for granted. "But I trust in You, O Lord; I say 'You are my God.' *My times are in your hands...*" (Psalm 31:14-15a)

During the lock-downs we were no longer able to meet with people face to face and share time together over a tea or coffee. It can become very easy when our freedom and choices are taken from us – to focus on those things we no longer have.

As we covered in the message on praise, our worship and appreciation to God ensures we focus on what we do have 'in Christ.' We thank Him for all He is – and not just for all He has done. We need to continue to worship Jesus, thinking on those things He has blessed us with.

Paul the apostle said, "For I have learned to be content whatever the circumstances. I know what it is to be in need, and I know what it is to have plenty. *I have learned the secret of being content in any and every situation...*" (Philippians 4:11b-12a)

Staying home with more time, my prayer life increased, especially in intercession for those in authority, nations, communities and families and individuals. I was reminded of those occasions, when I had heard people say (who can no longer serve in active ways) "I can only pray these days." *"Only pray." – is the most powerful weapon that we have.*

Prayer crosses borders, continents, and time zones. God is Omnipresent. He is everywhere at the same time. He longs to hear and receive our prayers. Prayer must remain our top priority as a disciple of Jesus. Through prayer we build our relationship with God – we hear His voice and grow in our love for Him.

In those days, everything was stripped away. We could not meet with family and friends; weddings were cancelled and we heard of the heart-breaking scenario of people being unable to attend the funerals of their loved ones. Everyone lost something during the lockdowns and the on-going pandemic, and tragically, millions world-wide lost their lives to Covid 19.

I was reminded that *whatever is taken from us in the future – Jesus always remains.* He is our hope, and He will never leave us or forsake us. He is our rock, fortress and refuge in every raging storm and dark valley.

At the end of each year, I take a review of all the activities and ministries that I am involved with, including church, family, and other contacts.

In my mind, I lay them all down, and then ponder and pray about what to pick up again. This helps in preventing me from becoming over-busy or doing too many things, which can lead to unfinished tasks or not doing things well. If I feel it is a season to stop a certain activity or role, it releases the time to consider something new, that God may be calling me to.

Covid literally put everyone in the position, where they had to lay down all their roles, meetings, and activities for a while. Now we can start up again, we have all had the choice to make as to – '*do we continue on as we were – or make some changes?*'

I have not rushed back into everything I was doing pre-Covid – but continue to seek the Lord in this new season. In Ecclesiastes 3:1 we read, "There is a time for everything, and a season for every activity under heaven." Most importantly, we need to make time to meet with God in our daily devotional times.

Another key lesson I learnt from not being able to serve in my usual ministries in Church during the lockdowns – was it reminded me – *'my true worth, value, and identity must be in Jesus alone, and not in what I do or accomplish.'*

Although we are called by God to serve Him and others, *I must make my relationship with Jesus, and hearing His voice, my daily top priority.* We are to serve Jesus out of our love for Him.

The greatest challenge for all Churches during the pandemic, was that their buildings had to close – as did many other public places and businesses – to help prevent the spread of Covid in crowded places. Many Church services went online as people could no longer meet in person for worship and fellowship. However, many found new creative ways of serving and witnessing to their communities.

This experience gave me an empathy towards the persecuted Church, which I pray for regularly. Even before Covid, thousands of believers in Jesus Christ, in dozens of countries around the world, cannot meet without the risk of being attacked, discriminated against, imprisoned, or being falsely accused. Many, many more – do not even have a Church building to attend for Christian worship.

We are now able to gather freely in our premises, but for these dear brothers and sisters in Christ, they continue to face the challenge of how they can meet together – knowing they risk persecution. May we all continue to lift them in our prayers and be spurred on to live for the Lord through their example of faith and trust in Jesus – even in their suffering.

As we keep walking with Jesus, may we seize each day and make the most of every opportunity that He brings our way, to speak, act and live to His glory.

Back in 2020, households received a letter from the Prime Minister, Boris Johnson. One of the things he mentioned concerning the Covid pandemic was, "Things will get worse before they get better." Regardless of Covid, all of us will continue to face situations which will get worse before they get better. *In God's perfect plan for our lives, God's best is always yet to come! Waiting time is not wasted time in God's purposes.*

In the times of testing, He is refining our faith. "Even though I walk through the valley of the shadow of death, I will fear no evil, for You are with me, your rod and your staff, they comfort me. (Psalm 23:4)

Keep Walking … Keep your eyes on Jesus – He is the Author and Finisher of our faith.